Pebble® Plus

You'll Love Cockapoos

by Erin Edison

Gail Saunders-Smith PhD,
Consulting Editor

CAPSTONE PRESS
a capstone imprint

Pebble Plus is published by Capstone Press,
1710 Roe Crest Drive, North Mankato, Minnesota 56003
www.capstonepub.com

Library of Congress Cataloging-in-Publication Data
Edison, Erin.
  You'll love cockapoos / Erin Edison.
    pages cm.— (Favorite designer dogs)
  Includes bibliographical references and index.
  ISBN 978-1-4914-0569-7 (hb)—ISBN 978-1-4914-0603-8 (eb)—ISBN 978-1-4914-0637-3 (pb)
1. Cockapoo—Juvenile literature. I. Title.
SF429.C54E35 2014
  636.76—dc23   2014001500

Editorial Credits
Erika L. Shores, editor; Kyle Grenz, designer; Katy LaVigne, production specialist

Photo Credits
Alamy: Chuck Franklin, 21; Capstone Studio: Karon Dubke, cover, 7, 17, 19; Shutterstock: Brian Lasenby, 9, Caleb Foster, 15, Cynthia Kidwell, 1, Eric Isselee, 5 (bottom), WilleeCole, 5 (top); SuperStock: NaturePL, 11, Randi Hirschmann, 13

Design Elements
Shutterstock: Julynx

Note to Parents and Teachers

The Favorite Designer Dogs series supports national science standards related to life science. This book describes and illustrates cockapoos, a cross between a cocker spaniel and poodle. The images support early readers in understanding the text. The repetition of words and phrases helps early readers learn new words. This book also introduces early readers to subject-specific vocabulary words, which are defined in the Glossary section. Early readers may need assistance to read some words and to use the Table of Contents, Glossary, Read More, Internet Sites, and Index sections of the book.

Printed in the United States of America in North Mankato, Minnesota
042014   008087CGF14

Table of Contents

What Is a Cockapoo?

A cockapoo is a designer dog. Designer dogs are a mix of two breeds. A cockapoo is a blend of a cocker spaniel and a poodle.

cocker spaniel

poodle

5

Cockapoos share the best
parts of two breeds.
Poodles are smart and shed
very little hair. Cocker spaniels
are friendly pets.

The Cockapoo Look

Cockapoos are quick, sturdy dogs.

Their bodies and legs are strong.

They have medium to long ears
and large, brown eyes.

The poodle parent decides
a cockapoo's size. Teacups and
toys are the smallest poodles.
Miniatures are midsize poodles.
Standard poodles are the largest.

Cockapoos can be black, white, apricot, chocolate, or cream. Some cockapoos are a mix of colors. Their coats are silky soft and wavy.

Puppy Time

Newborn cockapoos have tight, curly hair. The hair gets looser as they grow. Puppies grow quickly. Cockapoos can live 14 to 18 years.

Caring for Cockapoos

Take your cockapoo for a checkup every year. Veterinarians give dogs vaccinations and check for health problems.

Cockapoos should eat twice a day. Dogs do best when they are fed at the same times each day.

A Perfect Pooch

Smart, sweet cockapoos want to please their owners. Cockapoos learn and follow commands easily.

Glossary

apricot—a light, brown-orange color

breed—a certain kind of animal within an animal group

chocolate—a dark brown color

coat—an animal's hair or fur

command—an order to do something

shed—to drop or fall off

sturdy—strong and firm

vaccination—a shot of medicine that protects animals from a disease

veterinarian—a doctor who treats sick or injured animals; veterinarians also help animals stay healthy

Read More

Owen, Ruth. *Cockapoos.* Designer Dogs. New York: PowerKids Press, 2013.

Shores, Erika L. *All About Poodles.* Dogs, Dogs, Dogs. North Mankato, Minn.: Capstone Press, 2013.

Wheeler, Jill C. *Cockapoos.* Dogs. Edina, Minn.: ABDO Pub., 2008.

Internet Sites

FactHound offers a safe, fun way to find Internet sites related to this book. All of the sites on FactHound have been researched by our staff.

Here's all you do:

Visit *www.facthound.com*

Type in this code: 9781491405697

 **Super-cool stuff!** Check out projects, games and lots more at **www.capstonekids.com**

Index

Word Count: 187

Grade: 1

Early-Intervention Level: 14